CLASSIC
CHRISTIANITY
STUDY
SERIES

A Closer Look at the Reality of the Resurrection

BOB GEORGE

HARVEST HOUSE PUBLISHERS
Eugene, Oregon 97402

A CLOSER LOOK AT THE THE REALITY OF THE RESURRECTION

Copyright © 1992 Harvest House Publishers
Eugene, Oregon 97402

ISBN 0-89081-950-5

Printed in the United States of America.

Contents

No Other
Foundation

As a person's physical growth is based on proper diet and exercise, so is the Christian's spiritual growth dependent on regular feeding upon the Word of God and application of its principles. With more false teaching, shifting opinions and general confusion in the world than ever before, Christians need a solid foundation upon which to base their beliefs and build their lives. The Word of God declares that Jesus Christ is that foundation of truth. Therefore, the emphasis of the Classic Christianity Study Series is in helping Christians discover for themselves what the Bible actually says about Christ.

These Bible study guides are uniquely prepared for this purpose. They are useful for the newborn, intermediate or mature Christian in that they begin with the fundamental and central question of who is Jesus Christ and then build upon that foundation in a logical and progressive manner. The Classic Christianity Study Series is also extremely flexible in that it can be used for individual or group study.

The Book of Acts tells us that the first Christians were "continually devoting themselves to the apostles' *teaching* and to *fellowship*, to the *breaking of bread* and to *prayer*" (Acts 2:42). The need for a proper balance in the Christian life is as real today as it was in the first century. The Classic Christianity Study Series has therefore been designed to incorporate all of these elements vital for spiritual growth.

For no man can lay a foundation other than the one which is laid, which is Jesus Christ (1 Corinthians 3:11).

Helpful Suggestions
As You Begin

1. Choosing a convenient time and location will help you to be consistent in your study.

2. Use a Bible that you are comfortable with.

3. Before beginning your study, always pray and ask God to quiet your heart and open your mind to understand the Scriptures.

4. Approach the Word of God with a learner's heart and a teachable spirit.

1

Giving His Life to You

Jesus said, "I came that they might have life, and might have it abundantly" (John 10:10). Yet the average professing Christian is saying, "There is nothing abundant about my life. I know my sins are forgiven and that I am going to heaven, but what about today! I still experience doubts, fears, frustrations, and defeat. Surely there must be something more to this Christian life."

There is and it comes from understanding the fulness of the gospel. Most people when asked, "What is your understanding of the gospel?" respond, "Christ died for my sins." This is only part of the gospel. Christ was also raised from the dead, and it is through His resurrection that we see the full gospel. The full gospel can be summed up like this:

> **Jesus Christ gave His life for us;**
> **so that He could give His life to us;**
> **so that He can live His life through us.**

Jesus Christ died giving His life for us. He was raised to give His life to us. It is because of this that we take a closer look at the reality of the resurrection.

Key Verse: John 10:10

The thief comes only to steal and kill and destroy; I have come that they may have life, and have it to the full.

---

1. According to this verse, why does the thief come?

2. Who do you think the "thief" refers to in this verse?

3. In contrast, what has Jesus come to do?

4. How does Jesus say that we can experience life here and today?

5. Is it your desire to experience life "to the full"?

6. In John 1:4 where is life to be found?

7. According to 1 John 5:11 where is eternal life to be found?

8. Could eternal life be found in Christ if He had not been raised from the dead?

9. Read the following verses and then summarize the central theme of the apostles' teaching in the book of Acts.

Acts 2:32

Acts 4:2

Acts 4:33

Acts 17:18

10. Why do you think the central theme of the apostles' teaching and preaching in the book of Acts was the resurrection of Jesus Christ?

11. In 1 Corinthians 15:14, what does Paul say about his preaching and our faith if Christ had not been raised from the dead?

12. Where would we be left if Christ had not been raised from the dead? (Corinthians 15:17)

13. Why is Christ's resurrection important to you and me according to 1 Corinthians 15:21,22?

The Resurrection and the Life

Jesus said to her, "I am the resurrection and the life. He who believes in me will live, even though he dies; and whoever lives and believes in me will never die. Do you believe this?" (John 11:25,26).

1. What did Christ claim about Himself?

2. Why do you think Jesus refers to Himself as both the resurrection and the life?

3. What does Jesus say will happen to those who believe in His name, even though they may die?

4. What does He say about those who live and believe in His name?

5. In John 14:19, what is the reason we will live?

6. Could we live and have eternal life apart from the resurrection of Jesus Christ?

7. Why do you think Jesus Christ was raised from the dead?

8. What is the full gospel according to 1 Corinthians 15:3,4?

9. How much of the gospel is someone functioning on if he believes it is only "Christ died for my sins"?

10. What part of the gospel is he missing?

11. Is it any wonder, then, that so many of us are missing the abundant life Jesus promised?

Many of us at least think we understand the meaning of the cross. When it comes to the meaning of the resurrection, however, our minds draw a blank. Somehow we overlook the obvious—resurrection is the restoration of life. Jesus Christ was raised from the dead so that we might have life. The good news of the gospel is not just that Christ came to die for you, but that He came to live in you! Jesus Christ did not come just to get men out of hell and into heaven; He came to get Himself out of heaven and into men!

2

Man's Need
for Life

If you were to ask a group of Christians, "What does it mean to be saved?" most would answer something like this: "Jesus died for the forgiveness of my sins, so there is a place for me in heaven when I die." While this answer is not wrong, it is incomplete. Jesus said, "I have come that they might have life, and have it to the full" (John 10:10). What kind of person needs life? Someone who is dead.

The problem of mankind is not just that we are sinners in need of forgiveness; it is that we are dead and in need of life. We are born into this world dead spiritually, separated from the life of God.

Key Verse: Romans 6:23

For the wages of sin is death, but the gift of God is eternal life in Christ Jesus our Lord.

1. What are the wages of sin?

2. What is the gift of God?

3. Where is this eternal life found?

4. What are we saved from?

5. What then is the real issue of salvation?

6. In Genesis 2:17 what did God say would happen to Adam and Eve if they ate from the tree of the knowledge of good and evil?

7. In Genesis 3:7, what happened to Adam and Eve when they ate the fruit?

8. Did they really die the moment they ate the fruit?

If so, how did they die?

9. What does God mean in Genesis 5:1 when He said Adam and Eve were born in His image?

10. In Genesis 5:3, whose image was Seth born in?

11. Whose image are we born into?

12. Is this image the one of Adam as he was created or after he had died spiritually?

13. Therefore, since we are born in the image of Adam, how do we come into this world, spiritually alive or dead?

14. In Romans 5:12, what entered the world through Adam?

15. What was the result of his sin?

16. What came to all men?

17. In Ephesians 2:1, how does God see you and me before we come to Christ?

Why?

18. How does Colossians 2:13 describe man?

19. What does a dead person need?

20. What does God do for those who are dead?

21. What did Paul conclude about himself in Romans 7:24?

22. What question did he ask?

Where are you? Are you still dead trying to make sense out of this life? Are you going to bed every night saying "Is this all there is to life? I get up, go to work, come home, watch TV, go to bed, get up and do the same thing every day. There has to be more to life than this!"

Have you ever crossed over from death to life? Have you accepted what Christ did for you on the cross and asked Him to come to live in you and give you life? If not, why not do it this very moment and start enjoying life for the first time ever!

3

The Ministry of the Holy Spirit

We have learned that man is dead and in need of life, and that Jesus Christ was raised from the dead so that we can have life. But how is this life imparted to us? John 6:63 tells us that the Spirit gives life, and in John 3:5 we learn that to enter the kingdom of God we must be born again of the Spirit of God. It is through the agency of the Holy Spirit that God imparts eternal life to us. Just as the Spirit of God raised Jesus from the dead, it is the Spirit of God that gives you and me life (Romans 8:11). Let's take a closer look at the ministry of the Holy Spirit to see how He enables Christ to give His life to us.

Who is the Holy Spirit?

Key Verse: Acts 5:3,4

Then Peter said, "Ananias, how is it that Satan has so filled your heart that you have lied to the Holy Spirit and have kept for yourself some of the money you received for the land? Didn't it belong to you before it was sold? And after it was sold, wasn't the money at your disposal? What made you think of doing such a thing? You have not lied to men but to God."

1. To whom did Peter say Ananias lied concerning the money he kept for himself?

2. To whom did Peter say Ananias had lied when he lied to the Holy Spirit?

3. What do you conclude that Peter is saying concerning the Holy Spirit?

The Third Person of the Trinity

The Holy Spirit is the third person of the Trinity, co-equal with God the Father and God the Son.

How do you see the Trinity declared in 2 Corinthians 13:14?

Another example in life of a trinity is seen in something as basic as water—H_2O. H_2O can be a liquid, a solid, or a vapor depending upon whether it is water, ice or steam. All are H_2O.

The same is true of an egg. It consists of a yolk, a white, and a shell. All three are considered the egg.

These illustrations are limited, but they help show how one essence can exist in three separate forms.

Some wise professor once said, "Anyone who denies the Trinity will lose his soul, and anyone who tries to understand the Trinity will lose his mind!" The Bible clearly declares that the Father is God, the Son is God, and the Holy Spirit is God. Yet Isaiah 43:10-11 declares there is only one God and that "Before Me there was no God formed, and there will be none after Me. I, even I, am the Lord; and there is no savior besides Me" (NASB).

Our finite minds cannot understand all that is involved in the mysteries of God. In light of the evidence, however, we have only two options: either the Bible is contradicting itself or the Father and the Son and the Holy Spirit are each and uniquely God. We must conclude, therefore, that the sum total of the three equals the one ($1 \times 1 \times 1 = 1$, not $1 + 1 + 1 = 3$).

Why Did the Holy Spirit Come?

But I tell you the truth: It is for your good that I am going away. Unless I go away, the Counselor will not come to you; but if I go, I will send him to you. When he comes, he will convict the world of guilt in regard to sin and righteousness and judgment: in regard to sin, because men do not believe in me; in regard to righteousness, because I am going to the Father, where you can see me no longer; and in regard to judgment, because the prince of this world now stands condemned.

"I have much more to say to you, more than you can now bear. But when he, the Spirit of truth, comes, he will guide you into all truth. He will not speak on his own; he will speak only what he hears, and he will tell you what is yet to come. He will bring glory to me by taking from what is mine and making it known to you (John 16:7-14).

1. Who did Jesus say He would send to us after He ascended into heaven?

2. What three things will the Holy Spirit or Counselor convict the world of?

3. What did Christ say was the world's sin?

4. What did Christ say concerning righteousness?

5. According to Philippians 3:8,9, where is righteousness found?

6. What has happened to Satan, the ruler of this world?

7. What does Jesus call the Holy Spirit in Acts 16:13?

8. What job does the Spirit of truth have in our lives?

9. What is the function of the Holy Spirit in Acts 16:16?

10. Why do you think the Holy Spirit points us to Jesus Christ?

11. According to John 1:4, where is life found?

12. How is new life given according to John 3:3-6?

13. What must we be born of to enter the kingdom of God?

14. Who gives us the life that is found in Jesus Christ according to John 6:63?

15. Is it possible to belong to Christ without having the Holy Spirit within you? (Romans 8:9)

The doctrine of the Holy Spirit is one of the most important doctrines in the Christian faith. The ministry of the Holy Spirit is God's method of enabling the living Christ to live His life in and through us. It is through the Holy Spirit that God imparts His very life to those who believe in His Son.

4

Salvation:
A Life and Death Issue

There is much confusion today in regard to the real full gospel. There is a full gospel but sadly, to our loss, we stop short of it. We stop with the first half—the cross, where the penalty for our sins was paid by Jesus, and reconciliation (the clearing of the debt) occurred between sinful man and Holy God.

Yet, if we stop at the cross and do not "continue in the faith," as Paul exhorted in Colossians 1, continuing on from the cross, through Christ's resurrection, we miss the main benefit which the Lord Jesus came to give us—*life!* We become the beneficiaries of forgiveness, but do not receive life to enable us to experience it. *Life!* The second half of the gospel.

Key Verse: Romans 5:10 (NASB)

For if while we were enemies, we were reconciled to God through the death of His Son, much more, having been reconciled, we shall be saved by His life.

---

1. What does it mean to be "reconciled"?

Briefly stated, reconciliation is defined as *making peace between enemies.*

2. When was mankind **reconciled** to God?

3. What kind of person reaches out to an enemy?

4. How was reconciliation accomplished?

Man is not saved by the death of Christ, but by the *life* of Christ:

Salvation is being made alive.

1. Once man was reconciled to God through the substitutionary death of His Son, Jesus Christ, on the cross, how then was it made possible for man to be **saved**?

2. What, then, is the significance of the resurrection?

If the verse quoted above, Romans 5:10, is a capsulation of the gospel, how may separate transactions are contained within it?

a) How are we reconciled?

b) How are we saved?

> *In reply Jesus declared, "I tell you the truth, no one can see the kingdom of God unless he is born again."*

> *"How can a man be born when he is old?"* Nicodemus asked.
> *"Surely he cannot enter a second time into his mother's womb to be
> born!"*
> *Jesus answered, "I tell you the truth, no one can enter the kingdom
> of God unless he is born of water and the Spirit. Flesh gives birth to
> flesh, but the Spirit gives birth to spirit"* (John 3:3-6).

1. What did Jesus say must occur before a man could see the kingdom of God?

2. Of what things did Jesus say a man must be born in order to enter the kingdom of God?

3. If spiritual birth relates to the spirit, then to what does being "born of water" relate?

**If a man is not first born of the flesh,
he cannot be born of the Spirit.**

> *"I tell you the truth, whoever hears my word and believes him who
> sent me has eternal life and will not be condemned; he has crossed over
> from death to life"* (John 5:24).

1. What is the possession of those who hear the words of Christ and believe God, the Father, who sent Him?

2. What else did Jesus say about those who receive eternal life?

3. According to this passage, what have we crossed over from?

4. What have we become the beneficiaries of, as a result?

> *But because of his great love for us, God, who is rich in mercy, made us alive with Christ even when we were dead in transgressions—it is by grace you have been saved* (Ephesians 2:4,5).

1. What is God rich in, according to the Scripture above?

2. When we were still in our transgressions, in what condition were we?

3. Because of His great love for us, what did God do for us?

4. At this point, are you beginning to understand why salvation is a life and death issue?

> *When you were dead in your sins and in the uncircumcision of your sinful nature, God made you alive with Christ. He forgave us all our sins* (Colossians 2:13).

1. When we were in our sins, what condition did we live in?

2. What kind of nature did we possess?

3. What happened in spite of the deadness of our sinful nature?

4. What did God do, through Christ, in regard to our sins?

5. How many of our sins did He forgive?

6. How many does that leave remaining for you to deal with?

> *Jesus said, "Because I live, you also will live"* (John 14:19b).

How is it possible, according to what Jesus said in the statement above, for man to live?

> *Jesus said to (Martha), "I am the resurrection and the life. He who believes in me will live, even though he dies"* (John 11:25).

1. In the above passage, what two things did Jesus claim to be?

2. What did Jesus promise in regard to those who believe in Him?

Praise be to the God and Father of our Lord Jesus Christ! In his great mercy he has given us new birth into a living hope through the resurrection of Jesus Christ from the dead, and into an inheritance that can never perish, spoil or fade—kept in heaven for you (1 Peter 1:3,4).

1. In His great mercy, what has God given us?

2. Through what is this "living hope" made possible?

3. From what was Jesus resurrected?

4. What kind of inheritance do we receive because of this "new birth"?

5. Where is this inheritance kept for us?

6. If this is true, then what is the importance of the resurrection of the Lord Jesus Christ in regard to believers?

5

Christin You,
Your Hope of Glory

There is no fact in Christian experience of greater importance than the profound truth that "Christ lives in" you (Galatians 2:20). Misunderstanding of this spiritual truth enslaves many Christians to the impossible task of trying to live the Christian life. The inevitable failure of such attempts brings them to the practical conclusion that Christianity does not work.

This lack of emphasis on the living Christ may explain why there is such a great contrast between the church of Jesus Christ today and His church of the first century. In J. B. Phillips' introduction to *Letters to Young Churches* he states:

> "The great difference between present-day Christianity and that of which we read in these letters [New Testament Epistles] is that to us it is primarily a performance; to them, it was a real experience. We are apt to reduce the Christian religion to a code or, at best, a rule of heart and life. To these men it is quite plainly the invasion of their lives by a new quality of life altogether. They do not hesitate to describe this as Christ living in them."

Key Verse: Colossians 1:27

To them [His saints] God has chosen to make known among the Gentiles the glorious riches of this mystery, which is Christ in you, the hope of glory.

---

1. What is the mystery that God chose to make known among the Gentiles?

2. According to the revelation of this mystery, where is Christ?

3. How is the knowledge of the mystery of "Christ in you" described?

4. What does "Christ in you" mean to you?

5. In Hebrews 6:19, how is the hope of the believer described?

6. How do believers exercise the hope that we have in Christ according to Hebrews 11:1?

7. According to that same Scripture, how is faith exercised?

> *I have been crucified with Christ and I no longer live, but Christ lives in me. The life I live in the body, I live by faith in the Son of God, who loved me and gave himself for me* (Galatians 2:20).

1. What does Galatians 2:20 say about your life if you have been "crucified with Christ"?

2. Who is it that lives in you?

3. How do we live these lives that are being lived out through our bodies?

4. Faith, by its very definition, must have an object—something or someone in which or in whom faith is placed. Who is the object of the Christian's faith?

5. In what regard does Christ, the Son of God, hold believers?

6. What is the measure of God's love for believers?

7. How is God's love demonstrated toward us in 1 John 4:10?

8. What kind of response should God's love for us naturally engender in us toward others (1 John 4:11)?

9. According to 1 John 4:12, how is God's love made complete?

10. How do we know that we live in Him and He in us, according to 1 John 4:13?

11. Why is it important, according to 1 John 4:17, that His love be made complete?

12. According to 1 John 4:19, why is it possible for believers to love God?

13. When the Spirit of God comes to live in the believer it means that the person of the Holy Spirit comes to dwell within him. Whose mind do believers have according to 1 Corinthians 2:16?

14. What does it mean to you to have the mind of Christ?

> *But I say, walk by the Spirit, and you will not carry out the desire of the flesh. For the flesh sets its desire against the Spirit, and the Spirit against the flesh; for these are in opposition to one another, so that you may not do the things that you please* (Galatians 5:16,17 NASB).

1. What is the flesh in opposition to?

2. How is it possible to resist the desires of the flesh?

3. According to Philippians 2:13, who is at work in you?

4. Whose will is carried out when we walk in the Spirit?

5. What type of behavior is produced when we walk in the Spirit?

> *Those who are in the flesh cannot please God. However, you are not in the flesh but in the Spirit, if indeed the Spirit of God dwells in you. But if anyone does not have the Spirit of Christ, he does not belong to Him* (Romans 8:8,9 NASB).

1. Who are those "controlled by the flesh"?

2. If you are in Christ and the Spirit of God lives in you, who are you controlled by?

3. What is truth regarding those who do not have the Spirit of Christ?

> *And you also were included in Christ when you heard the word of truth, the gospel of your salvation. Having believed, you were marked in him with a seal, the promised Holy Spirit, who is a deposit guaranteeing our inheritance until the redemption of those who are God's possession—to the praise of his glory* (Ephesians 1:13,14).

1. What happens to a person when he hears (and believes in his heart) the Word of truth?

2. What does it mean to you to be "included in Christ"?

3. Once we believe, how are we then marked or identified?

4. The Scripture indicates that this seal is in the form of a person. Who is that seal?

5. What does the Holy Spirit serve as in this regard?

6. What does the "deposit" of the Holy Spirit guarantee?

7. According to Ephesians 4:30, how long will this seal last?

> *It has been said that Jesus Christ did not come to earth to get men out of hell and into heaven, but to get Himself out of heaven and back into men.*
>
> *To the Jews, He said, "You diligently study the Scriptures because you think that by them you possess eternal life. These are the Scriptures that testify about me"* (John 5:39).
>
> *I will give you a new heart and put a new spirit in you; I will remove from you your heart of stone and give you a heart of flesh* (Ezekiel 36:26).

If you have trusted Christ, He has come to live in your heart just as He promised, and you are now the beneficiary of "Christ in you, your hope of glory." With the Spirit of God living inside, you are a brand new creation (which we'll learn more about in the following chapter), and you now have eternal life.

6

A Brand New Creation

Throughout church history, there have been many hindrances to the spread of the gospel of Jesus Christ. Obvious among these are other religious systems like humanism, Hinduism, Islam, and the like. But none of these more prominent brands of religion has presented a hindrance to the gospel of the magnitude of legalism. Yes, legalism! The "Thou shalt not!" and "if you do, God is going to get you!" mentality.

God has not called us to ritualistic religious observances or meaningless rules and regulations which, according to Colossians 2, are of no value against fleshly indulgence. No, He has called us to freedom and liberty—He has made us into a brand new creation and enabled us to enjoy a whole new quality of life that is ours through Christ Jesus.

Key Verse: 2 Corinthians 5:17

Therefore, if anyone is in Christ, he is a new creation; the old has gone, the new has come!

1. What have those who are in Christ become?

2. What does it mean to you to be a new creation?

Let's make sure we understand just what God, through the apostle Paul, is telling us. In the previous chapter, we studied the reality of "Christ in you, your hope of glory."

3. What does it mean to you to be "in Christ"?

4. What has happened to those who are "in Christ"?

5. According to the passage quoted above, "the old has gone". What does this mean according to Romans 6:6?

6. Now that the old is gone, what has taken its place?

Being made into a "new creation" is somewhat like the caterpillar that has emerged from its cocoon as a new creature—a butterfly. As a caterpillar, it views life from the ground up. As a butterfly, it views life from the sky downward. In the same way, as a new creature in Christ, you must begin to see yourself as God sees you.

When one looks at a butterfly, he doesn't say, "There's a converted worm." Although it originally was a worm, and it was converted, now it is a butterfly, a beautiful, graceful new creature. The same is true of God. He only sees you as a butterfly—His new creation in Christ. Although you may not always act like a "butterfly," the truth of the matter is you are never going to be a worm again.

Just as surely as there is tremendous meaning in the reality of being "in Christ," let's also make sure we understand some things about what being a new creation in Christ does not mean.

Though your spirit has come alive to God in Christ, your body and soul (your mind, emotions, and will) have not been born again (Romans 7:18-24). Maturity and renewing the mind in Christ are not instantaneous occurrences. There are natural processes involved (Romans 12:2; Philippians 3:12-14).

Galatians 5:16 is just as important for what it does not say as for what it does say: "But I say, walk by the Spirit, and you will not carry out the desire of the flesh" (NASB). This does not say that the desires of the flesh will go away! And finally, a study of Galatians 3:1-5 and Colossians 2:23 will quickly reveal that we have no more ability to keep the law following salvation than we did before.

Now, what does it mean to be a brand new creation in Christ?

> *We were therefore buried with him through baptism into death in order that, just as Christ was raised from the dead through the glory of the Father, we too may live a new life* (Romans 6:4).

1. In the Scripture above, what is it that has become new?

2. As we read John 3:16 and Romans 6:23, we see that believers have become partakers of a whole new quality of life. What kind of life do we receive?

How, you might ask, does receiving this eternal life make "new creations" out of believers? Let's keep going.

Romans 6:23a states: "For the wages of sin is death—..."

1. What did it say is the wages of sin?

2. What kind of death is this?

> *They are darkened in their understanding and separated from the life of God because of the ignorance that is in them due to the hardening of their hearts* (Ephesians 4:18).

Death is the absence of life; it is spiritual separation from God. Adam was the first and only man created spiritually alive to God.

1. What happened to Adam when he sinned, according to Genesis 2:17?

2. Therefore, what caused the Spirit of God to depart from Adam?

In speaking of the sacrificial death of Christ, 2 Corinthians 5:21 states: God made Him (Christ) who had no sin to be sin for us, so that in Him we might become the righteousness of God.

1. What does the verse above say about Jesus in regard to His own sin?

2. What did Jesus do for us in regard to sin?

3. How do believers attain the righteousness of God?

4. Jesus was the only man ever born alive spiritually. Though He volitionally laid down His life (John 10:17,18), what caused the Spirit of God to depart from Jesus?

5. Whose sins?

> *For you have been born again, not of perishable seed, but of imperishable, through the living and enduring Word of God* (1 Peter 1:23).

1. If you are in Christ, what has happened to you?

2. What are believers "born again" of?

3. What does "imperishable" mean?

> *Everyone who competes in the games goes into strict training. They do it to get a crown that will not last; but we do it to get a crown that will last forever* (1 Corinthians 9:25).

New Testament believers are indeed new creations. But to summarize and gain the full perspective on why this is true, let's look once again at these very important questions:

1. What was it that caused the Spirit of God to depart from Adam in the Garden of Eden?

2. Whose sin?

3. What was it that caused the Spirit of God to depart from Jesus at the cross?

4. Whose sins?

5. What is the only thing that can cause the Spirit of God to depart?

6. Therefore, why is it not possible for one who has been "born again" of the Spirit of God to volitionally or unvolitionally cause God's Spirit to depart from him?

7. Where are a believer's sins?

> *Therefore, we can be assured of our place in Christ, because God has said, "Never will I leave you; never will I forsake you"* (Hebrews 13:5b).

Again, what has made it possible for God's Spirit never to leave us nor forsake us?

> *Praise be to the God and Father of our Lord Jesus Christ! In his great mercy he has given us new birth into a living hope through the resurrection of Jesus Christ from the dead, and into an inheritance that can never perish, spoil or fade—kept in heaven for you, who through faith are shielded by God's power until the coming of the salvation that is ready to be revealed in the last time* (1 Peter 1:3-5).

1. In His great mercy, what has God given us?

2. What have we been born into?

3. How is that accomplished?

4. What was Jesus resurrected from?

5. What is true of our inheritance through Christ?

6. Where is this inheritance kept?

7. Could you lose something that is being kept for you in heaven?

8. Through faith what are believers shielded by?

There has never before been a man like you. The first Adam was created spiritually alive but perished through sin. The second Adam, Christ, was born spiritually alive and perished through sin.

But New Testament believers, you and I, were "born again" to a new quality of life—eternal life, incorruptible, imperishable! That's why you are a new creation! And that's news worth repeating!

7

The Righteousness of Christ

Not only have we been made a new creation in Christ, we have also been given the very righteousness of Christ. Salvation requires that we be totally righteous. Jesus said in Matthew 5:48, "Be perfect, therefore, as your heavenly Father is perfect." Only perfect righteousness will do. Since this is an impossibility for us, God in His mercy and love chose to make us righteous through Jesus Christ. "God made him who had no sin to be sin for us, so that in him we might become the righteousness of God" (2 Corinthians 5:21).

Key Verse: 2 Corinthians 5:21

God made him who had no sin to be sin for us, so that in him we might become the righteousness of God.

1. What did God make Jesus do for you and me?

2. When God's Word says that Jesus became sin for you, does that mean He lost His righteousness, or merely that He took upon Himself the guilt and punishment that you deserved?

3. Whose righteousness do we become?

4. Where is this righteousness found?

5. Can we have the righteousness of God apart from Christ?

This Is God's Doing . . .

We are constantly reminded in His Word that it is God's doing that we are in Christ and the recipients of the gift of His righteousness, holiness and redemption. Because it is God's righteousness, it is not subject to corruption. It is not a resource which we improve upon or add to or use up; neither can we be the cause of its erosion or destruction by our own doing. It is God's gift to us in Christ Jesus and is described in the Scriptures as a coat which we who are in Christ wear. . . .

> *"For all you who were baptized into Christ have clothed yourselves with Christ"* (Galatians 3:27).

1. How, then, is one clothed who has received Christ as his Savior and Lord?

2. What does God see when He looks on the believer?

> *It is because of him that you are in Christ Jesus, who has become for us wisdom from God—that is, our righteousness, holiness and redemption* (1 Corinthians 1:30).

1. In God's wisdom, what has Christ become for us?

2. Could we have become righteous and holy through our own self-efforts?

3. What does God say about this in Romans 3:20?

The Gift of Righteousness

It is obvious that the gift of God's righteousness to us was provided to correct our absence of righteousness, specifically, our unrighteousness. This unrighteousness, His Word tells us, was the result of the trespass of one man. By that trespass (see Genesis 2:15-17; 3:1ff) of one man, Adam, death came upon all men. Likewise, by the righteous act of one man, Jesus Christ, many will be made alive. The similarity ends there. The significance of this comparison is to be seen not in the similarity but in the contrast:

> *But the gift is not like the trespass. For if the many died by the trespass of the one man, how much more did God's grace and the gift that came by the grace of the one man, Jesus Christ, overflow to the many! Again, the gift of God is not like the result of the one man's sin: The judgment followed one sin and brought condemnation, but the gift followed many trespasses and brought justification. For if, by the trespass of the one man, death reigned through that one man, how much more will those who receive God's abundant provision of grace and of the gift of righteousness reign in life through the one man, Jesus Christ* (Romans 5:15-17).

Many died by the _____

_____ . Much more God's grace and gift overflowed to the many by the

_____ , _____ _____ . The gift of God is not

like the result of _____ . What did the judgment that followed

that one sin bring? _____ . What did the gift that followed many

trespasses bring? _____ . By the trespass of one man,

_____ reigned through _____ . Those who receive God's abundant provision of grace and the _____ of _____ will reign in life through _____ _____ _____ , _____ _____ .

God's Abundant Grace ...

For all that God has provided for us, He does not force anything upon us. What He provides, He wants us to receive with grateful hearts as an act of our free will. A group of programmed robots is not His idea of a body of "called-out" believers. What He does desire is the heart that comes in humble faith for His "abundant provision of grace."

That person who feels no need for God's gift of righteousness, whose heart does not stir in response to God's offer will not "reign in life through the one man, Jesus Christ."

> *If we claim to be without sin, we deceive ourselves and the truth is not in us. If we confess our sins, he is faithful and just and will forgive us our sins and purify us from all unrighteousness* (1 John 1:8-9).

1. According to 1 John 1:8, how can people deceive themselves?

2. If we claim to be without sin, Who is not in us?

3. Who is the truth according to God's Word?

4. If we claim to be without sin, would we come to God for His gift of righteousness in Jesus Christ?

5. If we claim to be without sin, will we "reign in life through the one man, Jesus Christ"?

6. Is the person described in verse 8 "in Christ" or "in Adam"?

7. What does verse 9 say is the answer for this person's problem?

8. What will God do for him if he agrees with God concerning his sins and unrighteousness?

9. From how much of his unrighteousness will God purify him?

10. Will he then still be "in Adam"?

11. Will he then be "a new creature in Christ Jesus"?

Salvation requires that man must be totally righteous. If he is to be reconciled to God, he will have fellowship with God, literally in God's presence, and therefore must be totally righteous. From where must man's righteousness come? The Scripture reveals that no one is righteous in God's eyes for "all have sinned and fall short of the glory of God" (Romans 3:23). It was necessary, therefore, for God to provide man's righteousness. This He did, providing us with the very righteousness of Christ.

> For in the gospel a righteousness from God is revealed, a righteous-
> ness that is by faith from first to last, just as it is written: "The
> righteous will live by faith" (Romans 1:17).

> *What is more, I consider everything a loss compared to the surpass-*
> *ing greatness of knowing Christ Jesus my Lord, for whose sake I have*
> *lost all things. I consider them rubbish, that I may gain Christ and be*
> *found in him, not having a righteousness of my own that comes from the*
> *law, but that which is through faith in Christ—the righteousness that*
> *comes from God and is by faith* (Philippians 3:8,9).

1. If you have the righteousness that comes from God, how righteous are you in God's eyes?

2. If your righteousness were anything less than that of Christ's righteousness, could you receive His salvation?

3. If you are a Christian, are you as righteous in God's eyes as Billy Graham?

4. If you are in Christ, are you as righteous in God's eyes as the apostle Paul?

5. If you are born again, are you as righteous in God's eyes as Jesus Christ?

6. If you are not as righteous in God's eyes as Jesus Christ, can you be a child of God? Why not?

Lord Jesus, we thank You that You have given to us the gift of Your righteousness. We acknowledge that in and of ourselves is no good thing. With Paul, we want to be found in You, not having a righteousness of our own that comes from the law, but that which is through faith in You—the righteousness that comes from God and is by faith. In your name we pray, Amen.

8

A
Brand New
Identity

A devout member of a Hindu sect was confronted with the claims of Christ. To him all life was sacred—a cow, an insect, a cobra. Yet he could not grasp the Christian concept that God actually visited this planet in the person of Jesus Christ.

One day while walking through a field, wrestling in his mind with this concept of God, he observed an ant hill that was in the path of a farmer plowing the field. Gripped with similar concern that you and I would feel for hundreds of people trapped inside a burning building, he wanted to warn them of the impending danger. But how? He could shout to them, but they would not hear. He could write to them, but they would be unable to read.

How then, could he communicate with the ants? Then the realization came. Out of sheer love he wished that he could become an ant. If this could have been possible, he could have warned them before it was too late.

Now, at last, he understood the Christian concept. God called to us, but we wouldn't listen. He wrote to us, but we refused to read. Out of sheer love, Jesus Christ—God Himself—stepped out of heaven, took on a body of human flesh, thus becoming totally identified with man, so that man, when restored to God's original plan and purpose through faith in Him, could again become totally identified with God.

Key Verse: John 1:1,2

In the beginning was the Word, and the Word was with God, and the Word was God. He was with God in the beginning (John 1:1,2).

1. In the beginning, where was the Word?

2. Who was the Word identified as being in the beginning?

The Word became flesh and made his dwelling among us. We have seen his glory, the glory of the One and Only, who came from the Father, full of grace and truth (John 1:14).

1. What happened to the Word?

2. Where did the Word dwell?

3. Who was "the One and Only, who came from the Father, full of grace and truth"?

As we determined in chapter 6, those who have trusted Christ have become a new creation. Thus, we have a brand new identity. We are totally identified with Christ.

What shall we say then? Are we to continue in sin that grace might increase? May it never be! How shall we who died to sin still live in it? Or do you not know that all of us who have been baptized into Christ Jesus have been baptized into His death? Therefore we have been buried with Him through baptism into death, in order that as Christ was raised from the dead through the glory of the Father, so we too might walk in newness of life (Romans 6:1-4, NASB).

1. If we have been baptized into Christ Jesus, what else have we been baptized into?

2. What occurred in our regard through baptism with Him into death?

We Are No Longer Under the Law

Before this faith came, we were held prisoners by the law, locked up until faith should be revealed. So the law was put in charge to lead us to Christ that we might be justified by faith. **Now that faith has come, we are no longer under the supervision of the law** (Galatians 3:23-25).

1. Before faith came, what were we held prisoners by?

2. For what purpose was the law "put in charge"?

3. What is the purpose for our being lead to Christ?

4. What part does the law now have with those in Christ?

Why?

According to God's Word, those who have become identified with Christ through faith are no longer under the supervision of the law. They are no longer "held prisoners" by the law, but are freed to walk in newness of life.

> *Do you not know, brothers—for I am speaking to men who know the law—that the law has authority over a man only as long as he lives? For example, **by law a married woman is bound to her husband as long as he is alive, but if her husband dies, she is released from the law of marriage. So then, if she marries another man while her husband is still alive, she is called an adulteress*** (Romans 7:1-3a).

1. How long does the law have authority over men?

2. In the example above, how long does a woman remain bound to or identified with her husband according to the law?

3. If the woman marries another man while her husband is still alive, what is she called?

4. According to the context of this passage, what would a person be called if he became identified with Christ, then returned to the law?

> *But if her husband dies, she is released from that law and is not an adulteress, even though she marries another man. So, my brothers, **you***

also died to the law through the body of Christ, that you might belong to another, to him who was raised from the dead, in order that we might bear fruit to God. For when we were controlled by the sinful nature, the sinful passions aroused by the law were at work in our bodies, so that we bore fruit for death (Romans 7:3b-5).

1. What happens, as far as the married woman is concerned, if her husband dies?

2. Why are believers no longer identified with the law?

3. With whom have believers become identified?

4. Who was it that was raised from the dead?

> *But now, by dying to what once bound us, we have been released from the law so that we serve in the new way of the Spirit, and not in the old way of the written code* (Romans 7:6).

1. By dying to the law, what has happened?

2. For what purpose have we been "released from the law"?

So, when a person comes to Christ and becomes a child of God he is no longer identified with the law, but with Christ.

> *For through the law I died to the law so that I might live for God* (Galatians 2:19).

1. How did we die to the law?

2. For what purpose did we die to the law?

> *But when the time had fully come, God sent his Son, born of a woman, born under law, to redeem those under law, that we might receive the full rights of sons. Because you are sons, God sent the Spirit of his Son into our hearts, the Spirit who calls out, "Abba, Father." So you are no longer a slave, but a son; and since you are a son, God has made you also an heir* (Galatians 4:4-7).

1. When God sent His Son into the world, how was He born?

2. What was the purpose of His birth?

3. What was the result for those who have come to Christ by faith?

4. Because believers have received a new identity as sons, where has the Spirit of His Son taken up residence?

5. What was our previous identity?

6. What is our new identity?

7. And since we are "sons" what else has God made us?

Until and unless believers begin to understand that they have **a brand new identity** as sons of the living God, they will never truly begin to understand *the finality of the cross . . .* and *the reality of the resurrection.*

9

Living Under Grace

In Christ we have become brand new creations with a brand new identity. And with this comes a brand new way of life. Before, we were totally controlled by the desires of our flesh and in total bondage to the law of sin and death. Today, however, we have a whole new motivation for living. Through the gift of life, Christ has set us free from the law of sin and death, and now we live under the grace of God.

Key Verse: Romans 6:14

For sin shall not be your master, because you are not under law, but under grace.

1. What will no longer be our master according to this verse?

2. What reason does it give for sin no longer being our master?

3. According to 1 Corinthians 15:56, what is the power of sin?

4. Living under the law, what are you under the power of?

5. What do you think is the only way to get out from under the power of sin?

6. As new creatures in Christ, what are we now living under?

7. What have we gained access to in Romans 5:2?

8. How have we gained access into the grace of God?

9. As children of God, what are we constantly standing in?

10. Because we stand in the grace of God, what does Peter tell us to do in 2 Peter 3:18?

Saved By Grace

1. How is a person saved according to Ephesians 2:8,9?

2. Can we boast that we earned or worked to receive grace?

3. How did God's grace come to us?

4. At the Jerusalem council, what was the apostles' proclamation concerning how we are saved? (Acts 15:11)

5. How have we been saved according to 2 Timothy 1:9?

6. In Whom did we receive this grace?

7. What would become of grace if we were saved by any other way than by the grace of God?

A New Way of Life

Grace is not only what saves us, but is also what sustains us in our daily lives. That is why Peter tells us to "grow in the grace and the knowledge of our Lord and Savior Jesus Christ" (2 Peter 3:18). Let's take a closer look at God's grace and learn that through it God has provided everything we need to experience an abundant life here and now.

1. What must we receive to reign in life according to Romans 5:17?

2. What has God freely given us in Christ? (Ephesians 1:6)

3. How does John 1:14 describe Jesus Christ?

4. Who must we turn to, therefore, to receive God's abundant provision of grace?

5. Can we have the grace of God apart from Christ?

6. In Galatians 5:4, Who do we alienate ourselves from when we try to be justified by law?

7. What does Paul describe this as?

8. For those who are trying to live by the law and not under grace, how are they living their lives according to Galatians 3:3?

9. In Galatians 2:21, can righteousness be gained through the law, or in other words, our human effort?

10. How do we receive the righteousness of Christ according to Romans 3:24?

11. If you have already been given the righteousness of Christ by grace, does it make much sense to continue to work for it?

12. How will knowing that you have the righteousness of Christ change how you live your life?

13. Does the grace of God give you a new motivation for living?

14. What made Paul what he was in Acts 15:10?

15. Was the grace of God without effect in Paul's life?

16. Will it be without effect in your life?

17. Paul claimed that he worked harder than all the rest. What did he attribute this to?

18. A common criticism concerning the grace of God is that it causes people to be lazy; that they will no longer carry out the work of the ministry. How does Paul's statement concerning the grace of God compare to this criticism?

19. Do you think Paul could have made this claim if he was working to gain God's acceptance (law), instead of allowing God's grace to work in him?

20. What did understanding the grace of God in all of its truth do for the Colossian Christians in Colossians 1:6?

Teaching Us To Say No

For the grace of God that brings salvation has appeared to all men. It teaches us to say "No" to ungodliness and worldly passions, and to live self-controlled, upright and godly lives in this present age, while we wait for the blessed hope—the glorious appearing of our great God and Savior, Jesus Christ, who gave himself for us to redeem us from all wickedness and to purify for himself a people that are his very own, eager to do what is good (Titus 2:11-14).

1. What appeared bringing salvation to all men?

2. What does the grace of God teach us to do?

3. What do we learn to say no to through the grace of God?

4. Apart from the grace of God, can we say no to ungodliness and worldly passions? What happens when we try to say no through obedience to the law or through our own human effort? (Romans 7:5)

5. How does the grace of God teach us to live?

6. What does God's grace make us eager to do?

7. In Hebrews 4:16, what are we to approach with confidence?

8. What will we find at the throne of grace?

9. What does this grace do in our time of need?

10. What does God's grace do in our lives according to Acts 20:32?

11. As we walk in grace through every circumstance of life what will we learn about the grace of God in our lives according to 2 Corinthians 12:9?

We have seen what it means to live under the grace of God. Like in all things when we are confronted with truth, we are also confronted with a decision. We can choose to continue to work out the Christian life through our own self-effort or obedience to the law, or we can choose to live under the grace of God.

Will you choose to live each day growing in the grace and knowledge of our Lord Jesus Christ?

We have been called as children of God to live under the grace of God. We have a brand new identity with a brand new way of life. No longer do we have to try to live the Christian life or try to earn God's acceptance. Today, we can trust the living Christ and allow His grace to teach us to say no to ungodliness and to live righteous, upright lives as we wait for the glorious appearing of Jesus Christ.

10

Led by
the Spirit

———

To some, the Christian life is a matter of imitating Jesus, or following in His footsteps. In each circumstance the question arises, "What would Jesus do if He were here?" As good as this may sound, all the "trying to be like Jesus" mindset can produce, however, is a Christian actor. It is just another way of trying to live up to the standard of the law, an impossibility for even the best of men. God did not call us to be actors or to follow a set of rules and regulations. He has written His laws on our hearts and has placed His Spirit within us, so that we could be led from within. In this chapter we will take a closer look at what it means to be led by the Spirit of God.

———

Key Verse: Galatians 5:18

But if you are led by the Spirit, you are not under law.

———

1. What does this verse say about those who are led by the Spirit?

2. What does Paul call those who are led by the Spirit in Romans 8:14?

3. As a child of God, how then are we to live; under the law or led by the Spirit of God?

An Internal Motivation

1. Under the new covenant, where did God say He would write His laws? (Hebrews 8:10)

2. In 2 Corinthians 3:3, Paul says that we are a letter from Christ. What did Christ use for His ink?

3. What did Christ use for His tablet?

4. What do you think Paul is referring to when he mentions ink and tablets of stone?

5. Where were the ten commandments written? (2 Corinthians 3:7)

6. What difference do you think Paul is showing between the old and new covenants?

Truth and Grace

1. How are we to worship God according to John 4:24?

2. What did the Holy Spirit come to do in John 16:13?

3. What is truth according to John 14:6?

4. What does Jesus say is truth in John 17:17?

5. Therefore, where will the Holy Spirit be leading you?

6. What is the function of the Holy Spirit according to John 16:14?

7. Not only does the Spirit of God lead us into all truth, what else does He enable us to understand? (1 Corinthians 2:12)

8. Are we able to understand those things freely given to us (grace) apart from God's Spirit? (1 Corinthians 2:9,10)

**The Spirit of God leads us into all truth
and enables us to understand the grace of God.**

Filled With the Life of Christ

*Do not get drunk on wine, which leads to debauchery. Instead, be
filled with the Spirit* (Ephesians 5:18).

1. What are we not suppose to do according to this verse?

2. If you are drunk with wine, what is controlling you?

3. Does it make much sense to be controlled by wine?

4. Instead, what are we to do?

5. How are we to be filled with all the fullness of God in Ephesians 3:19?

6. Can you be filled with all the fullness of God and not be filled with the Spirit?

7. What does it mean to be filled with the fullness of Christ according to
Ephesians 3:17-19?

8. If you are filled with the Spirit, what are you filled with an understanding of?

9. What conclusions did Paul come to about the fullness of the love of God in
Romans 8:35-39?

10. What will be the result of one being controlled by the love of Christ? (2 Corinthians 5:14,15)

11. What effect did Christ's love have on the apostle Paul? (verse 14)

12. In Romans 8:9, if the Spirit of God lives in you, what controls you?

13. How is the law summed up in Galatians 5:14?

14. How are we to live our lives according to Galatians 5:13?

15. If you are being led by the Spirit, will you be fulfilling the law of love?

To be filled with the Spirit means to be controlled by the love and grace of God that is found in Christ Jesus. It is only as we yield in complete abandonment to this truth that we can ever experience the fullness of God in our lives. A mind that is set firmly upon the love and grace of God will ultimately be controlled by the love and grace of God. "The mind of sinful man is death, but the mind controlled by the Spirit is life and peace" (Romans 8:6).

In the context of Ephesians 5:18, we are to be "continuously being filled" with the Spirit. This is a process that is clearly seen in the passage as it relates to being filled with wine. Filling yourself with wine will ultimately lead to your being controlled by wine. It will affect your mind to the point that it will ultimately control your speech, actions, and your reactions.

So it is with the Spirit. If you are led by the Spirit, you will be filled to the measure with the knowledge of His love for you and His love will be expressed through you to the world.

11

An Eternal Inheritance

When we were still under the law, before Christ became the mediator of a new covenant, we were slaves. In Galatians 3:23 Paul says, "Before this faith came we were held prisoners by the law, locked up until faith should be revealed." Because we could not be justifed by the works of the law (see Galatians 3:11a), we were slaves to the consequences of the law—"the wages of sin is death . . ." Now that has changed. Christ has set us free from sins committed under the law. "So you are no longer a slave, but a son; and since you are a son, God has made you also an heir" (Galatians 4:7).

Key Verse: Hebrews 9:15

For this reason Christ is the mediator of a new covenant, that those who are called may receive the promised eternal inheritance—now that He has died as a ransom to set them free from the sins committed under the first covenant.

1. What is Christ the mediator of?

2. What do those who are called receive?

3. What did Christ set us free from?

4. How did He set us free from our sins?

5. What is that first covenant commonly referred to as?

6. Are we as Christians now living under the first covenant or the new covenant?

7. What does Paul say that we no longer are in Galatians 4:7?

8. What is our new identity?

9. Because we are sons, what else has God made us?

> *Now if we are children, then we are heirs—heirs of God and co-heirs with Christ, if indeed we share in his sufferings in order that we may also share in his glory* (Romans 8:17).

1. What does God say is true of us if we are children of God?

2. What else are we?

Even though we may know we are heirs of God, many of us, however, don't know what our inheritance is. As a result, we live our lives in spiritual poverty.

A good illustration of this is seen in the true story of a west Texas farmer named Yates. Mr. Yates owned a lot of undeveloped land. He raised sheep, but he lived in poverty. It was during the Depression years and he was having difficulty even feeding and clothing his family.

As Mr. Yates was facing inevitable bankruptcy, an oil company approached him to request permission to drill for oil on his land. The oil company began drilling immediately. At 1,015 feet they discovered the largest oil deposit at the time on the North American continent—a deposit that produced 80,000 barrels of oil a day! At that time, oil was selling for about $3.00 per barrel. Overnight Mr. Yates became a billionaire. The amazing thing about this incident, though, was that Mr. Yates had been a billionaire ever since he first signed the papers on the land; he just hadn't known it!

There are many Christians who are living in the same identical situation spiritually. The day we came to the Lord Jesus Christ in saving faith, God gave us everything we could ever need to live rich, full lives, but many of us have never discovered the "riches of our inheritance" in Christ Jesus.

Our Inheritance in Christ

1. Justified—For all have sinned and fall short of the glory of God, and are justified freely by his grace through the redemption that came by Christ Jesus. For we maintain that a man is justified by faith apart from observing the law (Romans 3:23,24,28).

What does this verse say about what we have done?

What does this verse say has been done for us?

This was done for us through what?

How does the apostle Paul maintain that a man is justified?

2. Chosen by God—For he chose us in him before the creation of the world to be holy and blameless in his sight (Ephesians 1:4).

When did God choose to make those who were co-heirs with Christ "to be holy and blameless in His sight"?

Is it His work or our responsibility to make us "holy and blameless"?

3. Totally Forgiven—When you were dead in your sins and in the uncircumcision of your sinful nature, God made you alive with Christ. He forgave us all our sins, having canceled the written code, with its regulations, that was against us and that stood opposed to us; he took it away, nailing it to the cross (Colossians 2:13,14).

How did God make you alive with Christ?

What has become of the law that condemned us to death for our sins?

Do you believe that when you are "in Christ" you are totally forgiven?

Do you accept the reality of the truth that God has reconciled you to Him?

4. Saved through His Life—For if, when we were God's enemies, we were reconciled to him through the death of his Son, how much more, having been reconciled, shall we be saved through his life! (Romans 5:10).

The redemptive work of Christ has been made complete for (in) you when you, having been reconciled to God by the death of Christ, receive His life into your heart. Christ did not come into this world to forgive your sins; rather, the truth is He forgave all your sins so that He could give you His life! His Spirit—residing in your heart—this is the promise of your eternal inheritance, this is salvation!

When were we reconciled to God?

How were we reconciled?

Having been reconciled, how then are we saved?

5. Righteousness—God made him who had no sin to be sin for us, so that in him we might become the righteousness of God (2 Corinthians 5:21).

What did Christ become for you and me?

As a result, what are we made in Christ?

Two miracles of God's grace in one: 1) How could Jesus, pure, holy, blameless and set apart from sinners, become sin for me? 2) How could I, a sinner, become the righteousness of God? Amazing Grace, how sweet the sound!

6. Made Perfect—Because by one sacrifice he has made perfect forever those who are being made holy (Hebrews 10:14).

What have you been made?

For how long a period of time have you been made perfect?

How were you made perfect?

Did you do anything to make yourself perfect in God's sight?

7. Holy and Blameless—But now he has reconciled you by Christ's physical body through death to present you holy in his sight, without blemish and free from accusation (Colossians 1:22).

How have we been reconciled to God?

How then are we presented to God?

How does Paul describe being holy in God's sight?

How did we get to be holy, through what we have done or through what Christ has done?

8. Baptized into Christ—The body is a unit, though it is made up of many parts; and though all its parts are many, they form one body. So it is with Christ. For we were all baptized by one Spirit into one body—whether Jews or Greeks, slave or free—and we were all given the one Spirit to drink. But in fact God has arranged the parts in the body, every one of them, just as he wanted them to be (1 Corinthians 12:12,13,18).

How were you baptized into Christ's body?

You have thus become one of _____ _____ which form _____ _____ .

Whose body is it?

How has God arranged the parts of the body?

9. Sealed in Christ—And you also were included in Christ when you heard the word of truth, the gospel of your salvation. Having believed, you were marked in him with a seal, the promised Holy Spirit, who is a deposit guaranteeing our inheritance until the redemption of those who are God's possession—to the praise of his glory (Ephesians 1:13).

You were included in Christ when you heard the _____ , the

_____ ____ _____ _____ . Having

_____ , you were _____ _____ _____ _____ __

_____ , the promised _____ _____ . He is a _____

_____ your _____ until the

redemption of those who are God's possession—to the praise of His glory.

10. Hidden with Christ—For you died, and your life is now hidden with Christ in God (Colossians 3:3).

Where is your life now according to this verse?

11. Clothed with Christ—For all of you who were baptized into Christ have clothed yourselves with Christ (Galatians 3:27).

As a Christian, with whom are you clothed?

How would you describe the meaning of this? (See Romans 13:14; Philippians 3:9).

12. Complete in Christ—For in Christ all the fullness of the Deity lives in bodily form, and you have been given fullness in Christ, who is the head over every power and authority (Colossians 2:9-10).

How much of God dwells in Christ?

What have you been given in Christ?

Can you add to completeness?

13. Loved Perfectly—"As the Father has loved me, so have I loved you. Now remain in my love" (John 15:9).

> *"For I am convinced that neither angels nor demons, neither the present nor the future, nor any powers, neither height nor depth, nor anything else in all creation, will be able to separate us from the love of God that is in Christ Jesus our Lord" (Romans 3:38,39).*

How does Jesus say He loves you and me?

How much do you think God the Father loved Jesus His Son?

What did Paul say concerning the love of God?

The above verses are our inheritance in Christ. How will knowing your inheritance affect the way you live from day to day?

Peter begins his second letter with the wonderful news that, "His divine power has given us everything we need for life and godliness through our knowledge of him who called us by his own glory and goodness" (2 Peter 1:3). In Christ, we have everything we need. Recognize the riches that you have in Christ and begin living the abundant life that He has promised. We pray "that the eyes of your heart may be enlightened in order that you may know the hope to which he has called you, the riches of his glorious inheritance in the saints" (Ephesians 1:18). Thank You, Lord Jesus, for what You have done for me. Thank You for my redemption. Thank You for the forgiveness of all my sins. Thank You for Your Holy Spirit which You have given as a deposit guaranteeing my inheritance as a son of God and co-heir with You. Thank You that You are faithful to complete the work which You began in me.

In Your name I pray, Amen.

12

Access to the Throne of Grace

As children of God, we have been given all the rights and privileges that pertain to sonship. One of the greatest privileges we have is access to the throne of grace. Regardless of our circumstances, we can go boldly into the throne of grace calling God "Abba, Father."

Key Verse: Hebrews 4:16

Let us then approach the throne of grace with confidence, so that we may receive mercy and find grace to help us in our time of need.

---

1. What does the writer of Hebrews tell us to approach?

2. With what attitude are we to approach the throne of grace?

3. What gives us the ability to approach the throne of grace with confidence?

4. Who would you say sits on the throne of grace?

5. What is Jesus Christ full of according to John 1:14?

6. Based on this verse, what do you think we will find when we approach the throne of grace?

7. What does Hebrews 4:16 say that will we receive and find there?

8. What will this grace and mercy do for us?

9. Most of us think that when we approach God, we will be met with condemnation and punishment because of something we have done. How do the above verses compare to this thought?

Peace With God

> *Therefore, since we have been justified through faith, we have peace with God through our Lord Jesus Christ* (Romans 5:1).

1. How are we justified according to this verse?

2. Since we have been justified, what do we have with God?

3. Through Whom did this peace come?

4. According to Colossians 1:19,20, how did Christ make peace for us?

5. Now that we have peace through Christ's shed blood, do we need to see ourselves as God's enemy anymore?

6. In Colossians 1:21, what is the reason that we once considered ourselves enemies of God?

7. In 2 Corinthians 5:19, does God count our evil behavior (sins) against us?

8. Therefore, is there anything to fear in approaching the throne of grace?

9. According to Romans 8:15, did we receive a spirit that makes us a slave again to fear?

10. What Spirit did we receive?

11. Through the Spirit of Sonship, what do we cry out?

12. What are we, therefore; enemies or sons of God?

13. How do you think God is going to treat His children?

Approach the Throne

In him and through faith in him we may approach God with freedom and confidence (Ephesians 3:12).

1. Who gives the ability to approach God?

2. What attitudes does Christ's work on the cross allow us to approach God with?

3. In your own words describe what you think this freedom and confidence means?

An illustration to help us see what it means to approach God with confidence and freedom is that of little John-John Kennedy. During his dad's presidency, magazines often showed pictures of little John-John either in his dad's lap or crawling on the floor of the oval office while seemingly important political meetings were taking place. John-John never had to make an appointment to see his dad, nor did he have to go through security checks like everyone else. He bound into the oval office at anytime. Why? Because the president was John-John's dad. In the same way, we can bound into the throne of grace, because the One who is there is our Father. Jesus Christ cleared the way through His death by taking away our sins and freeing us from the fear of punishment. And then Christ provided the confidence to enter by making us sons through His resurrected life.

1. According to Hebrews 10:19, how should we enter the Most Holy Place?

2. With what attitude can we draw near to God according to Hebrews 10:22?

Do you have peace with God? Have you trusted in Christ's work on the cross on your behalf? Have you received Christ's life making you a child of God? If so, boldly approach the throne of grace. You have nothing to fear. Christ has taken away your sins, and He has made you a child of the living God.

13

Our Assurance

Jesus Christ laid down His life for you then, so that He could live in you today. He came so that we might have life. But how can we be sure that we have eternal life? What is the basis of our assurance of salvation? These are questions that most of us have asked at one time or another. God answers these through the testimony of His Word and through the testimony of His Spirit.

Key Verse: 1 John 5:11-13

And this is the testimony: God has given us eternal life, and this life is in his Son. He who has the Son has life; he who does not have the Son of God does not have life. I write these things to you who believe in the name of the Son of God so that you may know that you have eternal life.

1. What is God's testimony concerning eternal life?

2. Where is this eternal life?

3. What do you have if you have the Son?

4. If you do not have the Son, what else do you not have?

5. What is eternal life dependent upon then?

6. Why did John say he wrote these things to those who believe in the name of the Son of God?

7. So, if you have the Son, can you know, not hope for or wish, but know that you have eternal life?

Why?

8. What is our assurance according to Hebrews 13:5?

9. Based on this, is there anything we could do that would cause Christ to leave us?

10. What is the only thing that could cause the Spirit of God to leave you?

11. What has God done with all your sins?

12. Therefore, can your sin cause God's Spirit to leave you?

13. If it did, what would you have to conclude about the statement in Hebrews 13:5, "Never will I leave you, never will I forsake you"?

The Testimony of the Spirit

> *Because you are sons, God sent the Spirit of his Son into our hearts, the Spirit who calls out, "Abba, Father." So you are no longer a slave, but a son; and since you are a son, God has made you also an heir* (Galatians 4:6,7).

1. Because we are sons, what has God sent into our hearts?

2. What does the Spirit call out?

3. What does this verse say that we no longer are?

4. What are we?

5. Since we are sons, what else has God made us?

6. In Romans 8:16, what does the Spirit of God testify to our spirit that we are?

7. According to this verse, what would the Spirit of God testify to our spirit about when we are in the midst of sin or bad circumstances?

8. When do we need the assurance that we are children of God the most?

9. What can we count on for that assurance?

10. How do we know that we live in God and that He lives in us according to 1 John 4:13?

Our assurance of salvation is based both on the testimony of the Word of God and the testimony of His Spirit in our hearts. In whatever circumstance we find ourselves God's Word continues to bear witness that "if you have the Son, you have life," and the Spirit of God bears witness to our spirit that we are in fact children of God. You can *know* that you are saved.

Have you come to Christ for life? Jesus said, "I came that they might have life, and might have it abundantly" (John 10:10). If you do not know for sure that Christ lives in you, you can invite Him to do so right now. The following is a suggested prayer.

> Lord Jesus, I need You. Thank You for dying for the forgiveness of my sins. Thank You for offering me Your life. I now receive Your life and Your righteousness. Come into my heart. Take control of my life and make me the kind of person You want me to be.

If you were sincere when you prayed, the living Christ has come to dwell in your heart. You have been made alive together with Christ, you have eternal life, and all of your sins have been forgiven forever. You are beginning the great adventure for which you were created as a child of God.

> *Yet to all who received him, to those who believed in his name, he gave the right to become children of God* (John 1:12).